Against Forgetting

POPPY FOR REMEMBRANCE

Against Forgetting

War, Love, and After War

Denise David

❧

Shanti Arts Publishing
Brunswick, Maine

Against Forgetting
War, Love, and After War

Published by Shanti Arts Publishing
Interior and cover design by Shanti Arts Designs

Shanti Arts LLC
193 Hillside Road
Brunswick, Maine 04011

shantiarts.com

Cover image by Thomas Q / unsplash.com; image of
oak tree by Agris Robs, Wikimedia Commons; image of
blooming cherry tree by Henry & Co. / unsplash.com;
image of evergreen trees by Dan Otis / unsplash.com

Printed in the United States of America

ISBN: 978-1-951651-31-2 (softcover)

Library of Congress Control Number: 2020937360

For my dear family,
and for all the storytellers

CONTENTS

AFTER WAR

Acknowledgments

I wish to extend generous thanks to the editors of the following journals in which these poems first appeared, sometimes in an earlier version.

Earth's Daughters: She Persisted: "Lydia's Advice" (November 2018)

Halfway Down the Stairs: Nemesis: "Strangers in Las Vegas" (September 2018)

Persimmon Tree: "An Egg a Day" (spring 2018)

Still Point Arts Quarterly: Four Freedoms Reinterpreted: "The Man in the Tan Shirt" (fall 2018)

An earlier version of *Against Forgetting: War, Love, and After War* was named a 2019 Semi-Finalist in the Louis Award Competition sponsored by Concrete Wolf Press.

I would like to thank Christine Brooks Cote, founder of Shanti Arts Publishing, for her wonderful collaboration and her goal of bringing beautiful and compelling books into the world. I hope this collection meets her vision of creating "something we need in our lives."

PREFACE

These poems, a collection of narrative and persona poems, tell powerful stories that grew from research and interviews I did for a creative nonfiction project about the war bride experience of World War II. The voices in these poems would not bend to inclusion in my other project; they demanded to be heard on their own. Some of the poems have a gentle tone but reveal small explosions at the end. Others record the smaller moments that live in the shadow of the loud narrative we call history. They speak of personal experiences, but they move to universal significance, as poetry is wont to do, offering a glimpse at the humanity overlooked in history's tale.

I have fallen in love with so many of the characters in the collection, my own relatives among them, extraordinary-ordinary people. I am passionate about wanting these stories to be shared as a tribute to all the people involved, and as a way for all of us to understand in a deeper, more personal way the lives of those who lived through a monumental war.

This book is divided into three sections: "War," "Love," and "After War," with the poems arranged thematically in these sections. Even though the poems relate to World War II and its aftermath, they have relevance to today's headlines: the moral ambiguity of separating children from parents; the difficulties of immigrants' experiences; the importance of "paying attention;" the small acts of humanity in the midst of devastation; the often unseen importance of women's lives, including the near invisibility in history of the stories of the war brides. This collection provides a legacy of a war that will soon be lost to first hand recollection, stories of an earlier time recalled here in an intimate witnessing.

WAR

COURAGE OF THE OAK

AGAINST FORGETTING

Wet earth scent
in heavy blue rain air
summoning damp wool school days,
like Proust's crumb of madeleine,
oak windows stretched ceiling high,
facts piled in towers.

Maps uncoil from wooden dowels,
countries wear summer pastels,
pink, pale green, oceans always blue.
Black, rubber tipped pointer,
soft tap, tap, teacher taps
tracing alliances,
arcs of invasion,
the world remade.

But voices unheard
in history's roar,
gather, circle kitchen tables,
prop heads on elbows,
lean forward into memory's wash
and speak their stories,
lives lived in that long ago war.

A Father, a Son, and a War
—for Vince

Three quarters of a century ago it happened, this story of a father
and a son and a war. He is thin, straight-backed, this son, 93,
who signed up back then to fight for his country.

His words circle the fragile moment of a father's disapproval,
immigrant from Germany, calls Roosevelt a warmonger,
     and says to his son:
"You'll be fighting cousins, you know. Is that what you want?"

While this son sent to England waits, letters from his father collect
like rocks in his shoes as he stares at the sea until he meets a girl
who invites him to Christmas across the bay with her family.

She cries on the crossing, the ferry haunted by dazed soldier-ghosts
returning from Dunkirk. He wraps his coat around her,
thin cover from a world without order.

When the invasion begins, he crosses to France,
cold and rain soaked. In Germany, they liberate a camp,
his words brittle in the telling:

"It was unbelievable what I saw,
but my father would not listen.
How could a father not believe his own son?"

His head drops to his chest,
rolls quiet-slow,
back and forth.

His father long gone,
the question, a hawk,
circling above.

Moonlight Sonata

And what of that night,
Beethoven's sonata of earth's beauty
twisted without mercy into
bombers' moon cacophony,
hope burnt to ash.

Was it not enough to melt
the medieval cathedral,
leaden roof running in rivulets
down cobbled streets,
or to glow ancient stone walls red,
night of bombing with no end?

Lady Godiva perched
on her white steed,
hair streaming
over her frail form,
cannot help them:
thousands wander,
panic palpable,
her city in stunned collapse.

Nature and art crumble,
reason lost in dislocation,
alone the offering:
trembling hands curl
around steaming mugs of tea,
sweet and strong,
passed in communion,
one human to another.

*On 14 November 1940, the Luftwaffe launched a devastating
attack, codenamed Moonlight Sonata, on Coventry,
England. The word "coventrize" was coined by the Germans
to describe the complete annihilation of a city.

HOPE

—May 10, 1941

Hope hid underground
in Britain that night,
the longest night,
when skies rained fire
and the British Museum,
in a fight for its life,
was done at last.

Water gushes
from hoses
destroying what
fire has not;
ancient seeds
from China stored
five-hundred years
or more, soaked.

But tendrils of language,
gossamer word webs,
wrap around lotus seeds,
sprout them into life,
hope germinating
in the garden
of a story.

Fog of War

— *May 10, 1941*

The figure drops
from the fog,
wobbly doll
floating down
onto a moonlit
Scottish field.

The plane ablaze
in the distance,
farmer stands near,
pitchfork in hand.
The man, a German,
on a mission of peace,
he says, with
an urgent message.

He left Munich
the evening before,
left his wife, his young son,
flew a Messerschmitt,
navigating alone,
north above the Rhine,
a loop to the left
over a darkening North Sea,
startling beauty at end-of-day light,
before crashing into craggy Scottish terrain.

The farmer lowers
his pitchfork,
invites him into the cottage,
offers the man a seat near the fire
and a cup of tea to wait
until the Home Guard
barges through the door
taking the prisoner away.

*On May 10th, 1941, Rudolf Hess, a high-ranking Nazi
officer, flew alone to Scotland seeking to bargain for peace.
Adolf Hitler denied any knowledge of the mission.*

German Plane in the Back Garden

Sunday dinnertime,
door open to the back garden,
thin swath of afternoon light
across the kitchen floor.

She stands at the sink;
along the back fence
her shaggy-haired son
runs with the dog.

She hears the engine,
familiar sputter, rough and uneven,
shadow silhouette dark on the ground,
a plane too low in the sky.

Her child looks up,
shades his eyes;
without warning the plane lifts,
moving to the fields beyond.

Against an azure sky
two bombs drift downward.
"I could see his eyes, Mum.
A German was looking right at me.
Did you see?"

She saw.

Red Lipstick

Mr. Hitler did not like red lipstick,
banned it in Germany,
had his own ideas of perfect men,
and perfect women.

Did he know lipstick's power,
a complicated history,
worn by women of the evening,
and Cleopatra, and Queen Elizabeth I, and
Elizabeth Cady Stanton
at suffragette meetings?

Women in Britain spread
their lips creamy smooth
in deep defiant shades of red
and when it was scarce,
beetroot would do.

It was left to the women,
huddled in shelters
night after night,
to crawl out in the morning,
put on a bit of lipstick,
keep their dignity,
find courage,
show up.

ENGLAND 1941

My grandmother bends time
to nights darker than hope,
slit open with sirens like knives.
Young mother and three children
yanked from sleep
grope their way down
darkened stairs,
narrow path of light,
hands balance
along shaking walls,
fear heavy as a bad dream.

Outside under the full moon circle,
her voice a prayer, she tells them
run fast as you can.
White rabbits in night clothes
scamper across dew-wet grass,
drop into the shallow shelter,
under thin curve of corrugated metal
beneath a grassy mound,
where my grandmother's roses
used to bloom in pink burst of warm.

Planes swarm above,
thousand-fold buzz of bees,
bombs descend, whistle-shriek
added for terror before the thud.

As if the bloody bombs weren't bad enough,
says my grandmother, who hid
in a closet during thunderstorms;
Hell must be a loud place.
Like Mnemosyne, she preserves history.

Tea Time

Smoke bellowed dark
over Dunkirk when the army
escaped by the skin of its teeth;
now Singapore was lost,
the treasury low,
shadows graying hope.

We shall buy all the tea
in the world, Churchill says,
important as ammunition.
Troops shall have unlimited tea,
the old Benghazi and a boiling vessel,
junior man's duty to brew it up.

Put the kettle on
like at home,
nevermind, nevermind,
tea's up, balm for trauma.

Tea time ritual
embedded with the troops,
baffling to the Americans.

*In 1942, the British government purchased in order of weight:
bullets, tea, artillery shells, bombs, and explosives.

No One Does Not Show Up

She senses morning
before light breaks,

hears the dawn chorus,
wrens, blackbirds, robins,

looks to her children,
asleep after the long night of shelling.

The all-clear has not sounded,
but she must go to work;

No one does not show up,
and besides her family needs the money.

She is alone with the children;
her husband away in the army.

Winnie feels her mother's
light kiss on her forehead,

hears her warm-breath whisper,
"Don't get up yet, luv,"

before she disappears in the gray
morning mist, and none of them can cry

the women and children
on the home front.

TEA IN THE GERMAN BATTERY

They were boys really,
the English soldiers
in the German battery,
empty now, above Gold Beach.

Days after the assault,
the chill of French rain
seeping into them
along with the fear, of course.

A cup of tea would help
they thought,
like at home
make things a bit better,

but when they made the fire
they forgot the
munitions stored
in the back.

Concrete erupts, spewing rubble.
"Bloody hell," someone yells, and
they all jump back,
laughing like schoolboys,
the laugh of the spared.

*The German Batteries built by the Germans as part of
the Atlantic Wall were said to be nearly indestructible.*

THE PIED PIPER

She cannot breathe
at the station
when they climb
onto the train amidst
streams of other children;
millions sent away.
Her son waves, going on holiday,
his younger sister in tow,
scared by the crowds, the train,
leaving her mother.
Is it too late
to call them back?

Probably no more than a year
everyone tells her,
and that feels unbearable,
but everyone is wrong.
It is six years
before they return,
changed, unfamiliar
versions of themselves,
their childhoods tucked into
the rucksacks they carry.

She hugs them,
grateful they are safe,
but her arms will not
reach around her daughter and son.
Like the children following the Pied Piper,
she has lost them.

*Operation Pied Piper was the name given to the evacuation of
millions of children from the cities in Britain to avoid the bombing.

ZIPPO

My Dad had one. The Zippo lighter company
close to his hometown, just across the state line,
but once the war started, the company stopped
making lighters for civilians,
made them only for the troops,
lighters like the men, drafted for the military.

All the G.I's carried them, coveted them,
the black crackle lighters hinged on top with a chimney,
so as advertised, they lit in the wind,
lighting the Camels or Lucky Strikes
they all smoke—to relax, to calm down,
to pass time, the waiting of war.

My Dad liked Ernie Pyle, war correspondent,
how he talked with ordinary soldiers,
kneeling down, shaking loose
a cigarette from a pack,
offering a smoke and a light,
the Zippo closing with the distinctive click.

Pyle listened to their stories.
Got so he would give them a Zippo lighter,
American made and well designed.
A kind of thank you, he said.

Days after D-Day, Pyle walked the beach at Normandy,
ordinary objects from ordinary men collect in the tide line—
tooth brushes, letters, black plastic combs,
and no doubt Zippo lighters.

The Heart of a Stranger

The story, a stone worn smooth with telling,
her father hid them, two American soldiers, in the cellar,
German soldiers pounding on the door.
She watched them drag her father and her brother outside,
line them up against the garden wall;
she knew they were going to be shot.

Gilberte and her mother screamed and begged and cried.
It was the older German who told the others to stop.
Just take the prisoners, he said, *leave the family.*

We never knew why he did that,
she says, her round, girl face fuller now,
thick brown hair shortened to gray.
No way to understand
the heart of a stranger,
during war.

Une Seconde Vie

In the first world war,
he painted gray,
tamping down color
in a darkened world,
but when the Nazis
goose-stepped into Paris
and the world fractured
a second time,

Matisse retreated
to the south of France,
from a colorless world
of war, divorce, and
a cancer in his gut,
to a bed where he
painted with scissors,
as he called it,
making for himself
une seconde vie.

Even as Marguerite and Amelie,
mother and daughter,
join the French resistance
and are hauled into prison,
he drops like Icarus
onto the page,
in un-shadowed hues,

fears drenched in color
take shape on the page,
a healing beauty.

Dear Gertrude

How did you manage
to lease the house
in the south of France,
the house you said you bought,
but no mind, the house
with the vegetable gardens
and a terrace with a view of the mountains,
Switzerland in the distance,
but not so very distant, twenty miles or so.
Gardens and servants and a lovely house,
but you were advised to leave.

You went back to Paris to look
for your passports in the apartment,
but you found only your dog's pedigree papers.
The dog, your dog with the papers,
would always have rations;
humans and dogs favored
by pedigree in those days.
You chose not to leave,
two women, Jews in occupied France.
You were a genius,
you always said so,
and you found a way to stay,
but we wonder, Gertrude, just how?

Two Weeks Before the End

A letter, fragile, yellowed,
folded and refolded like an old map,
like they used to give out at the Esso station,
the ones she propped up on her lap,
her fingers tracing routes
while he drove the old Chevy,
a letter kept with her papers for seventy years,
words in uneven type, dark and light,
a trail of the lieutenant's hunt and peck cadence,
letter pounded out on an old Remington,
written to the wife of a soldier, the Irish kid,
the one who was always smiling.

The letter the lieutenant's offering:
he knew her husband well, one of the best liked boys,
one of the best soldiers in his platoon, and in the letter,
Sgt. Donnelly will be forever outside that small German town,
weeks away from the end, crossing carefully,
feet on soil, on grass, on the open field with no rifle shots
until there are, and seven men lay dead.

The lieutenant says I was near your husband,
a few feet away when he fell. He died immediately,
still firing when he was hit. Losing men when it's nearly over,
he struggles for meaning in the great gaps of white space,

so much harder, he says, and then, Let's hope that *we*,
crossed out, a rephrasing
people will not have to go through another war.

His words tumble through time to us,
reminder of that moment
when soldiers were young enough
to imagine they could do this for us.

*Thank you to Charlotte Donnelly McLaughlin for sharing the letter
that inspired this poem.*

LOVE

DELICATE CHERRY BLOSSOMS

WHITE HANKIES FLUTTER

—for the War Brides of World War II

They speak of it
like yesterday,
that day of leaving:
gaggles of young women
gathered on the decks of ships,
white hankies lofted onto the breeze
small birds fluttering,
long the good-bye of those
uncertain of return.

The double-funneled ship
sounds a throaty blast;
contrapuntal their voices
melodious, sweet, and clear
float into the air,
a rising anthem from childhood
of country, kin, and home,
and after the singing,
a silence so solemn,
they cannot lift their eyes:
What have I done?

Docks melt into the distance.
Wings fold, white hankies
dab eyes, collect sniffles,
muffle the sorrow of leaving
from this migration of women
launched onto the sea
to live as immigrants always have
between new land and old,
the hunger forever in the belly
for the place one is not.

The Situation

—May 10, 1940

When the British
came ashore
Icelanders called it
the blessed war:
sailors seasick from a rough crossing,
few maps and no clear plan,
asking crowds onshore
stand back a bit, if you please.

But with them came,
astandio, "the situation."
Icelandic women
liked the men
from another land,
who were clean,
treated them kindly.

The government
forbade fraternization,
called them prostitutes,
called them traitors,
called for an investigation,
foreign troops were taking their women.

But hundreds married the men,
who came from the sea,
great grand-daughters of the women,
we suppose, who waited, staring
through Iceland's blue clear light,
longing for change.

*332 Icelandic women married foreign soldiers
as a result of the occupation.

Government Issue

They were men from the movies,
bringing chewing gum, chocolate and hope,
sparking fun in streets gone gray,
wearing well-tailored uniforms
in a country mending and making do.
They smelled of Old Spice and Lifebouy soap,
a million and a half of them in England.

Most had never left their home state,
let alone crossed an ocean.
Seasick on the journey,
the chill of English rain
settling into their bones;
they were homesick.

They were loud and brash,
drank too much,
bragged and boasted
everything at home was much bigger and better,
lonely men waiting for war to begin.

No Fraternizing

At first, there was to be no fraternizing,
keep the troops and the locals separate,
but soldiers streamed into England
by the hundreds of thousands,
crowding into every nook and cranny.

The Yanks have invaded our country, people said.
They're loud and rude,
complain about everything,
have no manners,
flash their money around;
they are a cheeky lot.
Their trucks and tanks
are clogging the roads,
the pub has run out of beer.

A girl can't walk by them
without being embarrassed,
whistled at, made to feel foolish
with their vulgar comments.

The military needed to change the plan,
promote goodwill, encourage the British
to invite these boys to Sunday dinner,
and don't let the men go
empty-handed, they were told.
These people are starving.

Get the Red Cross to host dances,
with coffee and doughnuts.
Invite girls from nice families,
the war will end;
but we will need to remain friends.

MAY I MARRY YOUR DAUGHTER

They stand
at the bar
at the pub
up the road

where my granddad meets his mates
for a pint in the evening.

My Dad shakes a cigarette free
from his pack of Lucky Strikes.

Ta Chuck, says my granddad,
prefers Woodbines, but to be polite,
holds the cigarette to his lips,
while the Yank gives him a light.

Blue hazy smoke rises,
circles lazily in the dim lit pub
where men argue politics,
catch up on news.

My Dad has a question.
Thought maybe you did,
says my granddad.

I want to marry your daughter.
We love each other.
I will be a good husband.
I can promise you that.

My granddad's blue eyes
take the measure of the man:
She has a mind of her own that one, but if she's decided
I will not stand in the way of her happiness.

My mustering out money is set aside,
says my Dad, a man of his word.
If she is not happy,
she'll have a trip home.

Fair enough, says my granddad,
But if you don't make her happy, remember,
I still know how to shoot straight.

LETTER TO HIS PARENTS FROM HERS

Thank you for your recent letter,
for understanding our anxiety.
Our daughter, our only daughter, is young,
and rather sheltered I fear.

We always hoped she would marry
an English boy, stay close by,
not saying you will not be
a good husband.
Its just that, you know,
it is such a long way, and
we were hoping, as you may guess,
for something a bit easier.

They are young. Will they
find housing, a job, a good life?
So many homes here
were destroyed by bombs,
our own damaged in two hits,
only recently repaired.

We hope that you will do
what you can to help them,
find a place for our daughter
in your family.

Please take good care of her.

*Thanks to Robert Luskin for sharing the
letter from his mother's parents.

H.M.S. QUEEN MARY

Ship larger than the Titanic,
three red funnels atop majestic ebony,
a thousand times across
an unpredictable North Atlantic,
ship of glamour and glory,
film stars and royalty,
ship of dreams.

During the war, a ghost ship,
filmy gray silhouette against sea and sky,
zigzagging an evasive dance,
fifteen thousand soldiers at a time,
shortened the war by a year,
Churchill says,
a heroic ship.

And after the war, G.I. Brides
by the thousands
crowd her decks:
women who risk everything
for their new husbands
in America,
ship of dreams.

AN EGG A WEEK

—for Lyn

Her voice
delicate
cherry
blossom
syllables
falling.

An egg a week, she says.
During the war, in London,
that is what we had,
but when I told
the family of the American
I married,
they brushed my words
and me away.

They told me, you know,
we had rationing here, too.
They really had no idea
what we had been through.

It made me angry
when I first came
to this country;
they said I had
a chip on my shoulder.

ADVICE TO MOTHER-IN-LAW

English Brides to Learn American Cooking:

Tell her how to defrost the refrigerator
how to work the automatic gas stove
how to make waffles on the double griddle

Take her with you when you shop,
teach her how to buy the right way,
how to cook the American way.

A pudding basin is really a casserole
and there is no dish quite
as American as hot dogs.

If she makes unfavorable comparisons,
overlook them. She might be homesick,

and don't forget to tell her
they are called beets not beet roots.

AT LEAST YOU WERE NOT THE ENEMY
—for Jutta

At least you
were not the enemy,
Jutta from Leipsig says,
her university English,
even and precise.

After the war,
we were given
one chance to leave
before the Russians
took over.
All of us women
afraid to stay,
afraid to go,
but we rode the bus
through West Germany:
they spit at us,
called us bad words.

When I met my husband,
an American soldier,
we moved to San Francisco.
I was pregnant,
I was young,
I had a lot of trouble—
a tubal pregnancy,
a Jewish hospital,
with a doctor who asked:
What did you do
in Germany during
the war, Jutta?

I said nothing.
I thought he might kill me.
Those were the bad parts;
I am not ungrateful.

They Too Are Casualties

They, who step off the cliff,
ground slipping away in clouds
of whispered words,
misty promises of loving
and luring them across
an indifferent gray Atlantic.

The young woman,
skin pale as the moon,
waits, like unclaimed luggage
at the dock, for the soldier
she married on a rain-puddled
London day.

A stranger's hand
light as breath,
gentle dance partner,
guides her to a quiet corner
where she watches
lips form words,

hears the voice steady
and kind, until their meaning
stuns, a red-marked slap
on her cheek: *I am so sorry.*
He does not want you; he has
begun divorce proceedings.

Red Cross documents record,
in faded fountain-pen ink,
the transporting of war brides, noting:
more complicated than expected.

HOMESICKNESS

—for Hazel

Like Odysseus her life drains
in rivulets of homesickness,
when she first comes to live
at the edge of the prairie,
stark silence stretching
into blackness, a quiet so deep
she might drown.

She misses family and friends,
misses buildings and noise,
going to work, to dances,
running through streets
during air raids.
She misses the war,
if you can believe it.

In Canada, the abundance
of food overwhelms her.
She watches a woman
drop two eggs
on the kitchen floor
for the dogs to lap up.
She wants to scream,
longs for the rationing
back home, for the not
being able to have
whatever you want.

Tensile Strength

Thick brown paper packages, flattened and bent,
arrive at Christmas or near birthdays
secured with twine, ink lettering precise and distinctive,
contents listed on a green custom's sticker,
no room for surprises.

Enduring rough treatment,
overseas travel in the hold of a ship;
journeys abroad not easy in those days,
even for packages.

The smell and taste of home
thread connection,
tensile strength strong enough
to cross a wide ocean.

Like the Bones of an Unknown Horse

You do not know him they say,
who he is, the blood of his family,
like the bones of an unknown horse,
he is a foreigner.

But her butterfly spirit flew to him,
the stranger in uniform;
her family stared across the scape of Osaka,
wood and paper houses eaten by flames.

You will wear shame, they say,
if you marry this American.
You will be ours no longer
when he leaves you in disgrace,
Madame Butterfly.

But tucked inside her child self
was the heart of a rebellious girl,
who did not want her marriage arranged,
to obey first her father, then her husband
and finally her son, melting into invisibility,
becoming the lowest in the house, the wife.

She would marry for love,
unfold her wings and
even when America was not as she dreamed,
when she changed her name
from Chikado to Susie,
wore her silk kimono,
stitched delicately with cherry blossoms,
to meet his parents, and they insisted
she change, she did.

It broke her heart to leave Japan forever,
but like Himeji Castle, she survived the war;
the girl inside would not be silenced.
She was a heron taking flight.

KANSAS

—for George

Kansas boots and the stance of a man used to riding horses,
George wears a plaid shirt like warm coffee in chipped mugs
on a Saturday morning. We are connected. We are not family.
Our mothers are women from overseas, women who married
American soldiers during the war. George pours his story
              into my cup.

"My father's plane exploded in the French village
where she lived," he says, pulling out a black and white
              photograph:
his mother, beautiful, dark hair and the tilt of her head like
              a 1940's film star.
She worked in the hospital, watched his recovery,
and when he healed, they married, had a son they named
George, who his father carried gently, unsteadily,
for a month, until the war ended and he was sent home.

George and his mother followed a month later on a liberty ship,
the Zebulon B. Vance. "I got real sick on the ship," George says.
but he was not the only baby to become ill
              on a barely converted troop ship,
ill-equipped to transport seasick war brides and diapered babies.

His mother told him, many times, about the baby
in the bed next to him who died, blond-haired like George.
They wrapped him in sheets
and buried him at sea.

When they got to New York, George was put in the
hospital at Fort Hamilton. He pulls
out a copy of the telegram, words in pasted strips, sent to his
father those many years ago
when his father came in from the fields, knowing the
danger of telegrams, but thinking
maybe just a delay, until he read the words cold as winter:
"Come immediately;
recovery uncertain."

George was in the hospital for nine days, but he made it.
He and his mother traveled to
Kansas and did just fine. And many times, over the years,
his parents went back to France
to that little village they loved.

George wants to understand what happened on that ship.
He looks it up on the Internet. Six babies died.
He finds an article from a Board of Inquiry.
In those days, they blamed the women.

AFTER WAR

PEACE OF THE WHITE PINE,
THE UNITY OF LIFE

Stories Like Warm Icelandic Socks

Around Christmas
it begins,
the flood of books,
started during the war;
imports limited so
new books escape
all at once,
with spines stiff
and the smell of words
on their breath.
They settle in on Christmas Eve,
purring in beds at night
in a land where winters
stretch long and dark, and
everyone can read.

LIFE SENTENCE

He walks the unsteady
gait of an old man,
twenty-eight rounds
in the outside garden,
drinks air twice a day,
memorizes sky,
the single prisoner
at Spandau,
number Seven.

It is mostly his son
who comes once a month
for the one hour visit
to the man who flew alone
on a mission of peace
that came to him, he said,
in a dream. Lunatic benevolence,
Churchill called it, and says
forty years is enough.

Paperwork piles in stacks,
pleas for release,
but the Russians say no.
At 93, the prisoner
takes his life, and
we are left to wonder
how long will we
warm ourselves
at the campfires of hate.

*Hess was kept longer than any other prisoner in Spandau
prison in Berlin, for many years its solitary prisoner.*

THINGS WORSE THAN BOMBING

White placards loop
around their necks,
name and age,
like packages in the post.
They stand in a line
stretching from edge to edge
of the town hall
in the small English village,
evacuees from the city,
a brother and a sister.
He is six, she is four.
Each carries a satchel,
change of clothes,
pajamas and a toothbrush.

They wait to be chosen:
but a stranger barks,
Got no room.
Can't take but the one.
The little sister cries
when they unfold her hands
from her brother's thick fingers.
Fussing won't do, they tell her.
Lucky to be here, you are.

Sixty years later
she remembers
the clack of the trains,
the crowds, the confusion.
Memories collected like silt
at the bottom of the sea
stirred when psychologists conclude:
separation from parents
may be a shock
worse than bombing,
but she knew that all along.

ACCENT

Her joyful words
dancing along
British country lanes
twirling full in lavender fields
and trellis roses overgrown,
lost their loveliness

when she was not understood,
asked to repeat herself,
told we do not have caster sugar,
never heard of it,

or when a stare burning indifference
surrounded her like a reprimand
when she spoke,
melting her confidence like sugar in the rain.

She swallowed her words
and herself.
She began to disappear.

LYDIA'S ADVICE

—for Lydia

When he created an incident,
pretext for invasion, prisoners drugged,
dressed in stolen uniforms,
and massacred in Gleiwitz for Polish aggression,
Hitler told his generals no one would ask
if he told the truth, no matter how implausible.

During the war, Lydia lived in a village
outside Munich. When the Americans came,
after liberating Dachau, ten miles away,
she found out later, she wondered
what would they think—
starving villagers stealing food
from a pried-open German army depot,
piling food into baskets and wagons,
whatever they had.

Now, she swims every day
in the ocean north of Los Angeles
She does not mind the cold water.
"I swim to keep my head right," she says.

We sit near a pool in Las Vegas.
Lydia leans in and whispers:
"There is something you should know
about our hotel." I think maybe bed bugs
or cockroaches in the kitchen,
but instead she asks: "Do you hear that bird singing?"

"Yesterday," she says, "I look in all the trees,
to see the bird with such a beautiful song,
but I can not find it. So I ask one of the staff,
and he tells me, oh there is no bird. It is a recording,
but no one notices."

Lydia, looks me in the eye
through her enormous, round glasses,
and says with ninety two years of life in her pocket:
"You have to pay attention."

For Gilberte

—French War Bride

She was afraid of the water, could not swim, did not like
      boats or rafts,
things that separated her from the land.

She made her children learn to swim, calmed them when
      they complained,
shivering in the cold morning pool.

You must be able to save me, she joked. They laughed and
      said they would,
swimming as life guards, never knowing water fear.

She was eighty when she told them about the train, the one
      the Germans bombed,
the one she was riding on, the one that dropped over the bridge,

and she was lost in the cold river
until a stranger pulled her to the surface.

A story locked in a trunk
at the bottom of a river.

All Through the War and Ever Since
—for Jean and George

Jean was the girl
in the bright red dress,
who bubbled laughter
like uncorked champagne
when she danced
with the soldier,
Canadian, tall and trim,
a good dancer, even in army boots.

It was wartime.
She was a firefighter
and an air raid warden.
He was sent to North Africa
then Italy. In those days,
worry sharpened the senses.
She married him
in a church outside London,
in a gown borrowed
from the butcher's daughter.

After the war, she joined him in Canada;
they were married for seventy-five years.
Jean always said: Together
we were a good thing,
through all the ups and downs,
we always knew.

No one could explain
when they died peacefully
in their nineties,
six hours apart:
Royal Canadian Engineer,
War Bride.

ITALIAN WAR BRIDE FOUND
HANGED IN HOME: JUNE 9, 1946

The headline a jolt
from the time
when newspapers
report details freely:
clothesline and
a basement rafter.

Two months earlier,
Clara, young war bride,
travels to Calumet City,
bars and speakeasies
lining State Street,
to join her husband,
who works the night shift
at the steel mill.

They live with his family,
Clara is moody and homesick
so he rents a one-room apartment
from a family of Italian descent.
He says he did not know what else to do.

And we are left to wonder:
did she think of her family,
the smell of pines in Tuscany,
the Cathedral of San Lorenzo
on the piazza in Grosetto,
or was it the taste of salt air
from her home near the lip of the
clear blue sea?

She did not say.
She did not speak English.

War Brides

The story of women
who chanced hope

from over fifty countries,

Albania, Algeria, Armenia, Australia, Austria, Belgium,
Bulgaria, Burma, Canada, China, Czechoslovakia, Denmark,
Egypt, England, Estonia, Finland, France, Germany,

women who dared to fall

Greece, Hawaii, Hungary, Iceland, India, Iraq, Ireland,
Italy, Japan, Latvia, Libya, Lithuania, Luxembourg, Mexico,
Morocco, the Netherlands, New Zealand,

in love

Northern Ireland, Norway, Palestine, New Guinea, Papua,
Portugal, Puerto Rico, Romania, Russia, Scotland, South
Africa, Spain, Sweden, Switzerland, Syria, Turkey, Wales, the
West Indies, and Yugoslavia,

with men from across the sea

after a war of the world;
women who made the peace.

CURVE OF WOOD

Splint made of wood beautiful,
marriage of sculpture and utility,
beneath museum glass,
inexpensive and light,
assembled in parts
for injuries sure to come
when soldiers crossed the sea
in transports brimming with khaki.

Husband and wife, lovers of design,
Charles and Ray Eames glue wood
in thin layers, alternate grains,
malleable and strong.

And after the war,
they press wood again
into human dimension
creating a chair for everyone,
the chair for the century,
an American chair.

The Man in the Tan Shirt

He is short, the man
in the tan shirt, unremarkable,
ahead of me in the check-out line.
He does not drop the divider
separating our groceries,
tofu from pork chops,
nourishment for different lives,
and then he does.

I smile and nod.
He unloads my
almond milk, quinoa, and mango,
lifts them onto the black
moving belt, then drops
his story into my cart.

"I am 94," he says,
"shop for my wife
 and me every week."
 I smile and nod,
 civility a smooth mask.

"Two weeks ago," he says,
"I got talking to a woman.
 She asks if I was in the service.
 When I tell her Guadalcanal,
 she stares at me and says
 her husband was there.
 Said it was pretty rough."

"When I go to cash out,
 funniest thing," he says
 shaking his head,
"She's paid for my groceries.
 Ain't that somethin'
 after all these years?"

DISPLACED PERSON

She lived in the house next to ours,
a very old woman, I always thought,
her white hair circled in a braid
at the top of her head,
her rimless glasses more circles.
The grown-ups said
she was a Displaced Person,
who came here after the war.

I did not understand her when she spoke.
I was afraid of her strangeness.
She was always outside working,
sweeping, raking, watering,
digging in her garden with a hoe.
Her gray sweater, once her husband's,
with pockets too large drooping over her house dress;
her legs, peeling tree trunks
wrapped in strips of tan cloth.

Once I saw her hair unwound,
white hair, as long as Rapunzel's, let down,
falling over her shoulders to dry in the sun,
like when she was a young girl
in the Polish countryside I suppose.

When her garden, stretching to the river,
grows full to bursting, she beckons me,
"Come to fence, neighbor," she says,
pulling roots from the soil by magic,
an onion with dirt still clinging
and a clump of blood red radishes.
Handing them to me, she says, "Give to Mama,"
the loamy smell of earth surrounding her.

Strangers in Las Vegas

Beryl, blond and fearless, was a restless girl in Manchester, England during the war. She met an American soldier, married him and went to a new life in New York, then a push on to California, until the earthquake swallowed their house. They would not stay after that.

They moved to Colorado, stayed for nearly twenty-five years until he died. Her new husband is Mexican, a stranger like her. His English is not great, but they love to dance, and they don't like the cold so they head south to the Las Vegas desert.

Beryl, my mother's friend for forty-five years, letters and pictures link them, war brides from England, the ribbon of their native land wrapped around their friendship. When I take my mother on her first trip to Las Vegas, we fly over the desert. "Where's the green?" my mother asks. "Not like home." She means England. She wonders how Beryl how handles the heat.

"We go to Walmart," Beryl explains, she and Chad, to walk the aisles where cool air flows in rivers. I think Chad must be Beryl's husband. "Oh no. Chad is her little dog. Joe Say is her husband," my mother says. I suppose she means José. "Yes," my mother says, "Joe Say." She means no offence. The spelling throws her off.

I ask if the Walmart people mind Chad walking up and down the aisles, but my mother says no. Beryl tells them he is a working/walking/comfort dog. Sometimes she takes him to the Casino with her. It is cool and you can get a free drink. I don't ask.

The guide on the bus tour tells us the Welcome to Fabulous Las Vegas sign is copyrighted. No one can use it without permission. On this day, people stream slowly past the sign anchored on the median among fifty-eight white crosses, lanterns with candles, and pictures pasted on cardboard glued to sticks sunk into the desert sand. No one here talks about the shooting. They call it the incident; the incident is fresh. Not so fabulous today.

We have been back home a fortnight when Beryl gives my mother a call. She says José has left, told her he was taking the wolf to Los Angeles to be near his daughter, and then maybe back to Mexico. "He means the Greyhound bus," Beryl explains. She understands him after thirty years. Beryl tells my mother he has said it before, that he will leave, but this time when he says, "I go," she tells him to bloody well go then.

They divide the money from their bank account. He packs his things into two large suitcases and a few cardboard boxes. Beryl will not drive him. It is his idea. "Let him figure it out," she says. When the cab comes, the boxes will not fit. The driver shakes his head: "You shoulda said you had all this stuff. You need a bigger cab." José looks at Beryl. "You keep them?" he asks.

Beryl softens. "He's not been well. I think he wants to go back home to Mexico to die," she says. "You know, back to the town where he was born. His brother is still there. He can't see well, can't drive anymore and has all this trouble with his legs."

Beryl calls his daughter in California to see if he got there, to ask if she should send the boxes. She hears him in the background shouting: "I am happy." Exactly like him to do that, she thinks. She wants to shout back, "Well, so am I," but she doesn't.

Beryl is a fearless woman from Manchester, England. She will stay here in the sun. She thinks about how only one's first place is home, but this is where she will live. It is not home.

Voice on the Telephone

The telephone, black and squat,
waits frog-like on a doily covered table.
I am five, playing dolls at my friend's house.
I have never called my mother on the phone.

It is okay, her mother says. Call her. Ask her
if you can stay for dinner, she says,
handing me a too-big receiver and
her curled-edge book with numbers penciled in.

I wait in unknown grown-up-ness.
When my mother answers,
I hesitate, a gaping gap of quiet.
Her voice strange, the accent foreign, unfamiliar.

I say it is not my mother,
but I know it is,
and I know then that she is not quite
like everyone else, and neither am I.

Seeing the Same Place for the First Time

I am elegant, sitting tall, my nine year-old self
riding for the first time in a black hackney cab,
like in the movies, I think, up the Tyburn Road
in the country of my mother's stories.

We serve into the grove,
a cul-de-sac, houses tucked securely
around a green grass center
where my mother used to play, she tells us.
but it is early morning quiet,
fog thick as pea soup, my mother says,
softening the world.

My mother's high heels click on the stone pathway,
my brother and I, ducklings, follow
close behind in a world she knows,
but we do not. The metal door knocker thud, thuds.
Inside comes the voice: "Blimey, they're 'ere."

My grandmother, across the room,
plants her walking stick,
leans forward, lifts herself from the chair.
She looks frail and smaller than she does
in the black and white photographs in our album.

When she sees my mother,
her face crumples like paper,
her tears collect in a sob, and for the first time
I see the enormity of my mother's decision.

Silence

It is the unspeaking I fear.
Children who know nothing
of the country their mothers left,
a lethal silencing of women.

Daughters who did not ask;
sons who answer with careless
indifference. She was a war bride,
but I am not sure how she came over.
No, we never went back.
My dad never wanted to talk about the war;
it was a long time ago.

Hibaku Jumoku

Few trees survived
the Flash
of Hiroshima.

A white pine,
diminutive, enduring,
watered, tended,
turned gently to the sun
by five generations,
until the bonsai master
entrusts care to a country
half as old as the tree.

His grandsons travel
over miles and oceans
to see with their own eyes,
their grandfather's great gift,
but the arboretum curators
did not know the fullness of his gift;
he had not spoken to them
of Hibaku Jumoku,

Forgiveness
quiet
an ancient tree.

*Hibaku jumoku is the term for the "survivor trees," trees that
survived the atomic explosions at Hiroshima and Nagasaki.

ABOUT THE AUTHOR

DENISE DAVID is a teacher, writer, scholar, wife, mother, and grandmother, but before any of that she was born the daughter of a British war bride, and that has made all the difference.

SHANTI ARTS

NATURE ▪ ART ▪ SPIRIT

Please visit us online
to browse our entire book catalog,
including poetry collections and fiction,
books on travel, nature, healing, art,
photography, and more.

Also take a look at our highly
regarded art and literary journal,
Still Point Arts Quarterly, which
may be downloaded for free.

www.shantiarts.com

www.ingramcontent.com/pod-product-compliance
Lightning Source LLC
Chambersburg PA
CBRC090930090426
42742CB00006B/105